So Cute! Baby Animals

# Chicks

By Katlin Sarantou

Chicks like to explore.

Chicks like to stroll.

Chicks like to chirp.

Chicks like to kiss.

Chicks like to snuggle.

Chicks like to gather.

Chicks like to step.

Chicks like to play.

Chicks like to peck.

Chicks like to roam.

Chicks like to stretch.

Chicks like to look.

# Word List

| | | |
|---|---|---|
| Chicks | snuggle | roam |
| explore | gather | stretch |
| stroll | step | look |
| chirp | play | |
| kiss | peck | |

# 48 Words

Chicks like to explore.
Chicks like to stroll.
Chicks like to chirp.
Chicks like to kiss.
Chicks like to snuggle.
Chicks like to gather.
Chicks like to step.
Chicks like to play.
Chicks like to peck.
Chicks like to roam.
Chicks like to stretch.
Chicks like to look.

Cherry Blossom Press

Published in the United States of America by Cherry Lake Publishing Group
Ann Arbor, Michigan
www.cherrylakepublishing.com

Photo Credits: © Volodymyr BurdiakCover/Shutterstock.com, cover, 1; © Rov7/Shutterstock.com, 2; © otsphoto/Shutterstock.com, 3; © Catalin Rusnac/Shutterstock.com, 4; © Richard Peterson/Shutterstock.com, 5; © Santirat Praeknokkaew/Shutterstock.com, 6; © KRIACHKO OLEKSII/Shutterstock.com, 7; © 6493866629/Shutterstock.com, 8; © Tomsickova Tatyana/Shutterstock.com, 9; © MilousSK/Shutterstock.com, 10; © Santirat Praeknokkaew/Shutterstock.com, 11, 13; © Elena_Goncharova/Shutterstock.com, 12; © WildlifeWorld/Shutterstock.com, 14, back cover



**Cherry Blossom Press** is an imprint of Cherry Lake Publishing Group.

Library of Congress Cataloging-in-Publication Data

Names: Sarantou, Katlin, author.
Title: Chicks / by Katlin Sarantou.
Description: Ann Arbor, Michigan : Cherry Lake Publishing, [2021] | Series: So cute! baby animals | Audience: Grades K-1 | Summary: "Aww. How cute! Early readers will learn about what chicks like to do. The simple text makes it easy for children to engage in reading. Books use the Whole Language approach to literacy, a combination of sight words and repetition that builds recognition and confidence. Bold, colorful photographs correlate directly to the text to help guide readers through the book"– Provided by publisher.
Identifiers: LCCN 2020032509 (print) | LCCN 2020032510 (ebook) | ISBN 9781534179905 (paperback) | ISBN 9781534180918 (pdf) | ISBN 9781534182622 (ebook)
Subjects: LCSH: Chicks–Juvenile literature.
Classification: LCC SF498.4 .S27 2021 (print) | LCC SF498.4 (ebook) | DDC 636.5–dc23
LC record available at https://lccn.loc.gov/2020032509
LC ebook record available at https://lccn.loc.gov/2020032510

Printed in the United States of America
Corporate Graphics